SEASON

o f

DARES

SEASON *of* DARES

LEAH SILVIEUS

BULL★CITY
PRESS

DURHAM, NORTH CAROLINA

Season *of* Dares

Published in the United States of America

Library of Congress Cataloging-in-Publication Data

Silvieus, Leah
Season of Dares: poems / by Leah Silvieus
p.   cm.
ISBN-13: 978-1-4951-7879-5

Book design by Spock and Associates

Cover photograph by Reed Silvieus
Author photograph by Roque Nonini

Published by
BULL CITY PRESS
1217 Odyssey Drive
Durham, NC 27713

www.BullCityPress.com

CONTENTS

For my mother, Mary Silvieus, and my grandmothers,
Mary Wanda Little and Laura Silvieus

In memory of Dr. Pamela Corpron Parker (1959-2016)

A VISION

The summer I turned twelve, the age that was,
      by some unknown angel's arithmetic, the year

            of accountability, I waded down through
      the sticky sweet cottonwoods to the river

and rose up, anointed. So forgive me if I speak now
      as I did then, as a child—mouth full

            of split-rail, rust, riverstone—
      I witnessed the spirit descending

among the ridges teethed with flame: *prepare ye,*
      prepare ye the way of the horde.

EQUINOX

Our house begins to crawl
           with wasp heads,
    budding like beads

from holes in the ponderosa walls.
           The intruders
    patrol our sills,

creep through bed sheets,
           sting us in sleep.
    They lord over the sandbox birch;

their colonies hover, thunderheads
           from our eaves.
    At dusk, father douses

their branch with gasoline.
           We bat the nest down
    with sticks, tear

through the coil, delicate
           as pastry in our fingers.
    In their folds, evidence

of our lives: wisps of garden
           mud, pulp filched
    from pine beams,

winding through the inner whorl
                of paper, a strand
        from the house's darkest head, mine.

ELEGY FOR DAYLIGHT

Midsummer's 10 o'clock dusk had us
ditching swings, twisty slide 'n jungle gym
for the beyond. Boneyard. Field. Forest.
The mountain ash's galaxy of orange berries
that stung hard as BBs if you knew how
to put a spin on 'em. Ducking behind
gutted-out combines 'n coils of chicken wire,
we counted each scrape 'n scab testament
to grit, tough shit, or consequence—scraped up
seed potatoes with sticks 'n fingernails
fooling ourselves they were gold enough
to buy our way out of town. As night tucked in,
our harvest turned to dirt-clod fights:
a little spit and dirt

> could make some mud
> hide a stone
> hide a bruise

our skin
welted but unbroken—

WHEN ASKED WHERE I'M (REALLY) FROM

"To be Asian in America is to be quizzed, constantly, about your ethnicity. What are you? Where are you from? No, but where are your parents from?"

– Jeff Guo, *The Washington Post*

Between two halves
  of a canyon's split lip,

    whose namesake the streets sing—
  all that is holy

after opening day
  of hunting season: Remington,

    Winchester, Pistol
Drive. Full of sandstone

'n gunpowder.
  No-stoplight town

    always taking,
two kids, at least, each year:

pulled under by river snag,
  by huffing Krylon Gold,

    accident of gorge's curve
or gunshot. If asked,

I'll tell you:
        not where I'm from

                but where I was made: wanting
        nothing but escape,

the only girl who knew
        how to play—called to accompany

                wherever there was need.
        Bye, Bye

Birdie auditions, weddings
        & Lutheran ladies' Christmas teas,

                I was the girl who could
        sight-read a melody

but always had trouble
        keeping time, whose door

        a mother'd come knocking on
in the middle of the night,

asking for a song.

THE WORLD JUST NOW, EMERGING

after the storm and the stillness that came before,
      we make our way down to the river,

past the autumn burn pile and the first stirrings
      of the birds in the apple tree.

My husband untangles himself from his winter woolens
      and lopes ahead, having known too much

of paradise to resist cold's threat,
      his back a fevered kite

tearing down the pale field:
      for each of his steps

two of my own, heavy
      through the crisp lip of snow

as if a haul from some deep well,
      and I wonder if it will always be this way—

him forging ahead as I lose sight in the gray tangle
      of creeper and paper birch,

calling his name as if he were miles
      away and not a few paces,

reckless in my panic
        as I thrash through the brush,

afraid he will not wait,
        afraid I will leave him, waiting

ANIMAL MEDICINE

The pit bull's been pacing for days, gazing out
the screen door at ghost rabbits in the pasture,
circling around again, whimpering. He can't
understand the cost of finally belonging

to someone, of healing from so many years of neglect.
Three injections of melarsomine in three months,
deep in the hip, and we're only on the first round.
It's heartworms, so the alternative is agony:

larvae then a white skein of parasites threading
the arteries of the lungs before the heart
finally fails. Years ago in Tallahassee, I stood
in the black box theater, watching you direct

auditions for *This Property is Condemned*. I never saw you
so gentle. Pacing upstage, downstage. Begin at the end
and run all the way through. Unremarkable to watch
at first, then how the boy and girl began to soften,

each gesture yielding response, a sort of living-in.
I watched as they became Alva, became Owen—
but it was never about us. The beautiful sister was always
going to die. The worms will be gone by spring.

MARYLAND ROUTE 210 DUSK

It's the third or fourth
body this week. You've lost

count. Hard to tell from afar, first
mistaken for shredded tire

or garbage fallen from trucks
that only today, a week after

the blizzard, are running again.
You've come to learn

the shape of them, the way they lie
along the shoulder of the highway,

legs curled to abdomen, as if just borne
into the world. The body tonight

is not a man, though from fifty yards
it could have been, front legs thrown

around his head as if to shield
himself from a blow.

Tonight, this body does not belong
to a man but to a dog—

soft and well-cared for, the kind
that has a name written

on the collar you'd find
if you'd just pull over.

You don't.

Dead, already, you reason.
Besides, it's dangerous to stop

even for a moment
in these dark and rushing hours;

no one would stop for you
or the shape of you, inseparable

from the body you'd be hunched over
as headlights swept past you,

filing toward well-lit homes.

SO BLONDE

it's almost white, I insisted the August
I convinced my best friend my hair turned gold
in the sun. That summer I was fooling whoever'd listen,
had Brandy and Crystal and Jessie believing
I heard Hanged Nelly giggle from a bathroom stall
& swore I was my mother's natural born daughter,
just came out looking like this, *a genetic anomaly.*
Most of them believed me for a minute or longer
& sometimes I almost did, too—imagined a lilting
headful of tousled blonde, light as my baby brother's.
Pale enough the public pool tinted it green. Mine,
thick & black, so coarse when trimmed, the ends
splintered bare feet. An unruly animal my mother
brushed daily—detangled & laced into days
of pigtails & braids, made me a pretty second
to the chestnut blonde Mormon twins
in French & Dutch plaits, headband halos
and fishtails—before I refused to brush my hair
& conjured myself *a rat's nest,* but O how I loved
my horde of snarled darlings, so dark, so generous
of fur & tail & teeth.

FIELD ELEGY

We carry the fawn down to the woods,
the body still light and lifelike, as if
it still carried some of the spirit,

this animal, which only hours before had been crying
for its mother, abandoned in an open field.
I sit with the fawn as my new husband digs,

striking roots and rocks until he finds a soft place
where the soil has some give. I can't stop
touching the small, pink wound in its spotted side

or the belly, still soft and damp with sweat beneath
a ribcage just bigger than my fist. I fold the slender legs
neatly as if bedding it down and he lowers the body

into the hole, just deep enough to keep the dogs
from dragging the carcass back to the house.
I flinch as the body topples over, its hooves tangling

in oak roots. Even though I know the suffering is over,
I want to shut its round, black eye,
now dulling as it stares up through the soil—

I want to make it look as if it were sleeping
and not dead—as if such a thing were a mercy
to this fawn and not to me, now alone

in this field and bleating.

ON THE FEAST OF EPIPHANY

Tonight, the valley in lunar glow,
    the maples' darkboned host fishes visions

from ice. There is no marker but an invisible line
    dividing night from night, snow from snow.

There are no directions to the closest lighthouse, no signpost
    to tell how far from shore. As children here,

our mothers coaxed our tongues into prayers
    for mild winters and taught us to cull from them deliverance:

deer strung cruciform from shed rafters, cold blood cherries
    filling the cellar. We learned to play dead, knotting our hands

behind our necks to protect from grizzlies, to chisel
    breath-space in avalanche and trail the North Star home.

Tonight, my brother studies clouds, tells me
    the storm will break next morning. Once, I too could divine

first snow, but tonight, the heavens refuse me. The firmament
    rolls over, dreaming of other prophets.

SELF-PORTRAIT AS SECRET-HEART-OF-GOLD BOY

Never forget your anger, baby, a man once said to me, *that's where your power lies.* And I mistook this recognition for love, having always wanted to hold the two of them in the same hand—anger and power—like the boys in the movies I didn't know if I wanted or wanted to be. Busted-lip, chip shouldered boys: Jimmys, Tylers, Keiths, and Codys. Blue jean, black leather, always white. Guitar-riffed and bass-driven, crowd-parting boys swaggering into auto shop, locker room, guts of a flickering mall. Secret-Heart-of-Gold boys starving for their chance at glory—anointed Son, Bud, Untapped Potential, cooling off on the sidelines after a ref's bad call. Not the Good Girl I was, back of the ladies choir bus, bubblegum-glossed and glittering like a scream. How I prayed to wake up believed-in. Deserving. Swinging fists the maverick teacher calms just before the credits—*I see you.* And having been seen, he is therefore transfigured: boy turned endless field, turned stadium at sunset, a burning multitude of men believing their empire will never stop winning.

AFTER EASTER

Of course, the flowers were dead
to begin with, cut as they were,
but three days after Easter,
they've begun to rot and Pastor Mark
jokes the church smells like a funeral.
Why shouldn't it? Christ may have risen,
but nothing lasts forever.
I walk the sanctuary, pull stems
from murky vases, brush petals
from the choir loft. This year,
the lilies, named after dead
saints or the *glory of God*, refused
to open, despite trying to force
their blooms with hairdryers.
Back home, Easter had everyone
in our town driving the dim hours
to the houses of the dying for sunrise
service, the early hours clawing up
our throats as we sang *Up From the Grave
He Arose* into the bluing hills. I'd run
into the weeds, gorge on fistfuls
of sugar birds, and dare our dead Christ
to rise from my green body.

AUBADE WITH SEPTIC FIELD

The morning you leave, the willow oak chokes
        the septic lines, filling the tub and sinks with shit.

The plumber shows me this on his small camera:
        the gunky tunnel throat-like, slick with slime

and almost fleshly, sinker roots strangling
        the central pipe. A tree's roots, he says, can reach

as wide as its crown but it's impossible to tell
        from the surface. All summer the tree bloomed

three yards from our door, brushing our eaves
        with catkins. And just beyond the septic field

a dying stretch of grass behind the shed, a grave
        unmarked for our spoil. The day before you left,

the tree woke us, shrieking with grackles. If only
        we'd asked the birds, they would have told us

this does not happen overnight—each day we cave
        a little more, eave by lichen, pipe by crown

giving ourselves over to what's entangled
        us long underground.

PRAYER TO SAINT MARTHA

Late August the galley blooms
        fruit flies, smoke-winged & garnet-eyed, circling
the over-sweet caves

of pear & blueberry, clingstone
                peach. Each night I pray resurrection

        but am deceived. Faith is not feast
but desire, not beauty of the table but what drags us starving there—

        what was buried inside
the sweetness—pearl-bright larvae within

the plum's rotten core. Saint dear
        of my difficult hunger:

                cloy me
                        mote me

        rise me up

PAROUSIA

Long enough abandoned, a place becomes an elsewhere:
purple knapweed wilding the arches of the sunken
church, stone angels haloed in tillandsia, where
sometime between our leaving and return,
magpies perched and shat
until something grew.

MATTHEW 19:14

after Jericho Brown

for the camp girls

Heaven belongs to such as these
        your apostle taught us,

so Lord, let me not forget:
        those six Julys

of girlhood summers down
        that two-lane highway, left—past

the seven-foot, plastic Hereford bull
        at Clearwater Junction; sleeping

in cast-off army tents
        where forty-miles-away might've

been a different country, those
        faraway towns' names exotic:

Philipsburg, Frenchtown,
        Wisdom, Choteau—

bless those mouths red
        with Fla-Vor-Ice, singing

rise and shine and give God the glory,
        glory. As we waited

for the mess tent dinner bell
   the counselors decreed,

the last shall be first
   and the first shall be last

and we all turned 'round in line
   'cause we believed

that one day it'd be true.
   Lord forget us not in our hour

of need—those who dug Dixie cups
   from trash bins to tear into visions

of the Blessed Virgin, who stole change from Right to Life
   coin banks to buy Ring Pops for little sisters.

Bless us, Lord, we dirt-road orphans, grown now
   as we are and miles from the closest home—

girls once named after virtues
   our mothers hoped we'd hold true:

Faith, Joy, daughter after daughter
   called Mercy.

ACKNOWLEDGEMENTS

I am grateful for those publications in which many of these poems first appeared:

AAWW's *The Margins*: "*So blonde*"

Anomaly: "Elegy for Daylight" and "Matthew 19:14"

diode: "After Easter" and "On the Feast of Epiphany"

Four Way Review: "Prayer to Saint Martha"

Hyphen magazine: "Field Elegy"

Melusine: "Equinox"

storySouth: "The World Just Now, Emerging"

Washington Square Review: "Aubade with Septic Field"

wildness: "When Asked Where I'm (Really) From"

Special thanks to Jessica Marion Modi and Sacred Americas Folio editor Desiree C. Bailey.

My deepest love and gratitude to those people and communities who have walked alongside me as these poems made, and sometimes clawed, their way into the world: to Kundiman, the Voices of Our Nations Arts Foundation, to Jericho Brown and my fantastic family at Tin House Summer Workshop, the folks at the MFA program at the University of Miami including M. Evelina Galang, Maureen Seaton, Mia Leonin, John Murillo—and to Lee Herrick, who supported me from afar. Thanks to Mr. E and Mr. W for their constant support and encouragement. To Bull City Press, Leslie Sainz, and Ross White for believing in this manuscript and their vision. To my brilliant *Hyphen* magazine family of constant cheerleaders. To my adoptee sisters for their support and vulnerability: Marci Calabretta Cancio-Bello, Ansley Moon, and Tiana Nobile. Love to my creative community whose companionship, couch-crashing sessions, and conversations I could not survive without: Carl Adair, Jessica Borusky, Kate DeBolt, Rachel Gray, Phil Lacey, Hannah Oberman-Breindel, and Kent Szlauderbach. To Justin, my truest blue. To my family who's always believed in me, even when I read books through entire family camping trips and didn't brush my hair. To Sean who makes me happy.

This collection is dedicated to Dr. Pamela Corpron Parker, to whom I owe my first steps into the world as a writer—for her mentorship, friendship, and encouragement to trust my own voice—or, as Aurora Leigh might say, to "write my story for my better self." Thank you.

ABOUT THE AUTHOR

Born in South Korea and raised in Montana and Colorado, LEAH SILVIEUS now travels between Florida and New York as a yacht chief stewardess. She is the author of *Anemochory* (Hyacinth Girl Press, 2016) and her debut full-length collection, a finalist for the Kundiman, Orison Books, and Agape Editions prizes, is forthcoming from Sundress Publications in 2019. She is a Kundiman fellow and has received awards from The Academy of American Poets, Fulbright, the Voices of Our Nations Arts Foundation, and U.S. Poets in Mexico. She holds an MFA from the University of Miami and a BA from Whitworth University.